Exploration

Rebecca Heddle

OXFORD
UNIVERSITY PRESS

OXFORD
UNIVERSITY PRESS

Great Clarendon Street, Oxford OX2 6DP

Oxford University Press is a department of the University of Oxford.
It furthers the University's objective of excellence in research, scholarship,
and education by publishing worldwide in

Oxford New York

Auckland Bangkok Buenos Aires Cape Town Chennai
Dar es Salaam Delhi Hong Kong Istanbul Karachi Kolkata
Kuala Lumpur Madrid Melbourne Mexico City Mumbai
Nairobi São Paulo Shanghai Taipei Tokyo Toronto

Oxford is a registered trade mark of Oxford University Press
in the UK and in certain other countries

Published in the United Kingdom
by Oxford University Press

First published 2001
10 9 8 7 6 5 4

British Library Cataloguing in Publication Data

Data available

ISBN 0 19 917451 2

Also available in packs

Explorers and Discoveries Inspection Pack (one of each book) ISBN 0 19 917452 0
Explorers and Discoveries Class Pack (six of each book) ISBN 0 19 917453 9

Acknowledgements

The Publisher would like to thank the following for permission to reproduce photographs:

AFP: p 30 (bottom); Bridgeman Art Library /Collection of Andrew McIntosh Patrick: p 26 (left); Bridgeman Art Library / Down House,Dowe, Kent: p 14; Bridgeman Art Library/National Library of Australia: p 10; Bridgeman Art Library/Natural History Museum: p 11 (top); Bridgeman Art Library/Private Collection: p 9 (top), Bridgeman Art Library / Wolverhampton Art Gallery: p 18 (left); Corbis: p 28 (right); Corbis/A.I.S.A.: p 22 (top left); Corbis/Bettmann: pp 6/7, 12 (top), 12/13, 16 (bottom right), 22 (main and title page), 26 (right); Corbis/David Cummings/Eye Ubiquitous: p 5 (top); Corbis/Historical Picture Archive: p 16 (bottom left); Corbis/Robert Holmes: p 25 (bottom); Corbis/Kennan Ward: p 20 (middle); Corbis/Kimbell Art Museum: p 5 (bottom); Corbis/NASA: p 13; Corbis/Roger Ressmeyer: pp 21, 27 (right), 28 (left); Corbis/Jeffrey L Rotman: p 27 (left); Corbis/Keren Su: p 6 (left); Corbis/Jim Sugar Photography: pp 25 (top left), 29 (bottom); Corbis/Ralph White: p 23 (top); Corbis/Adam Woolfitt: p 22 (top right); Corel Professional Photos: p 4 (bottom left), 15 (both); H M Bark Endeavour Foundation Pty Ltd: p 11 (bottom); Hulton Getty: pp 4 (bottom right), 18 (right), 19 (top), 20 (top left & right); Jason Lewis: p 30 (top); NOAA: p 29 (top); P A Photos: p 23 (bottom); Popperfoto: p 19 (bottom); Royal Geographical Society Picture Library: p 25 (top right); Scala: pp 16/17, 17 (right).

Front Cover: Photodisc Inc.
Back cover: Bridgeman Art Library

Illustrated by: Kathy Baxendale, Stefan Chabluk, David Cusik, Richard Morris and Tony Morris.

Designed by Alicia Howard at Tangerine Tiger

Printed in Hong Kong

Contents

Why go exploring?

The history of exploration is a story of curiosity and bravery. Explorers past and present have gone on their travels for many different reasons. In the past, some went to open up trade routes. Others wanted to solve scientific problems, or travelled for political reasons to benefit their country. Whatever the reason, there were often dangers to face and difficulties to overcome. This book looks at some of the most important explorers, why they went on their travels, and the different challenges they faced.

▶ Many famous historical journeys of exploration were made across uncharted oceans by sailing ship. We have now begun to explore beneath the oceans, in special underwater vessels, and out into space, travelling by rocket-powered spacecraft.

▲ **Astronauts** have a long training. They have to get themselves fit and learn to use complicated equipment and computers. Since the first magnetic compass, exploration has always involved the development and testing of new technology.

▲ Exploring new places often means having to get around in unusual ways, as these tourists discovered in Egypt around 1910.

1 Going to new places

Travel for religion

One of the first explorers we know about was a Chinese Buddhist monk called Hsuan-tsang. He wanted to find out more about his religion. He knew Buddhism had come to China from India, and in 629 AD, he asked the Emperor for permission to investigate.

The Emperor refused because he didn't want anyone to travel outside China. But Hsuan-tsang ignored the Emperor. He travelled right across China and India, and back home again, on a journey that lasted 16 years. His life was often in danger on the journey.

▲ Indian statue of Buddha

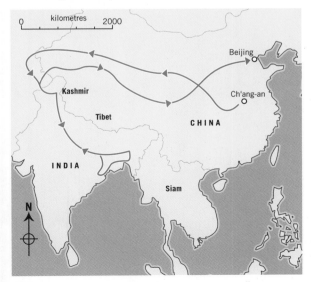

▲ The route Hsuan-tsang took from China to India and back

The Emperor forgave Hsuan-tsang for disobeying him. The monk brought home 700 religious books, and statues and relics of Buddha. Hsuan-tsang translated many of the books and is still remembered as a very important Chinese teacher of Buddhism.

▲ Chinese statue of Buddha

Exploring for trade

Christopher Columbus set out from Spain in 1492 to find a new route to India and the Far East. People from Western Europe wanted to get to the East to bring back valuable silk and spices.

A new route to the East was needed because powerful Muslim rulers would not allow Christian traders to use the old, overland route which went across their countries.

▼ Spices were highly valued, as they were used for flavouring and preserving food.

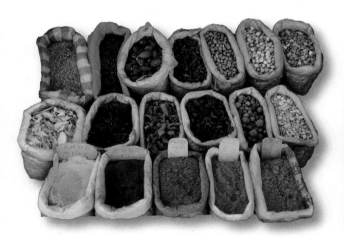

FACT

Before people had fridges, food went bad easily and often tasted horrible.

Columbus's great idea

While other explorers looked at the possibility of sailing to the East around Africa, Columbus wanted to sail westwards, and round the world. Like most Europeans, Columbus thought the globe was much smaller than it actually is – and did not know America existed.

▼ Columbus took three ships: the *Pinta*, the *Niña*, and the *Santa Maria*. They landed in the Bahamas, in the Caribbean, on 12 October 1492.

▼ Columbus thought he could sail round the globe like this.

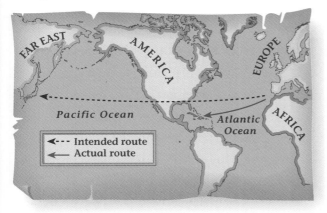

▼ In fact, this is where he went.

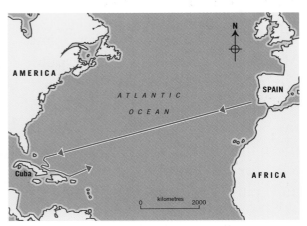

Columbus came from Genoa, in Italy, but his **expedition** was **sponsored** by the King and Queen of Spain. Like Columbus, they hoped to become rich from the new **trade route** *(see p.18).*

On the voyage, Columbus's ships had to travel out of sight of land. This was an alarming experience for his sailors, who were used to finding their way by following the coast. They threatened to take over the ships and sail back home, but Columbus persuaded them to continue for a little longer. Fortunately, they soon landed on an island off the mainland of America.

A new world

Columbus hoped his journey would be important for trade, but his accidental "discovery" of a new **continent** had even more importance. It changed the way people thought, both about the world and their own place in it.

Is it possible?

The Portugese **navigator**, Ferdinand Magellan, wanted to look for a route around South America to Asia. Was such a voyage possible? He persuaded the Spanish to send him, promising to make them rich and powerful by finding a new **trade route** to the Spice Islands (now part of Indonesia).

Magellan set off from Spain in 1519, with five ships and 237 men. They sailed across the Atlantic and down the coast of South America, where one of the ships was wrecked. The other four sailed to the Pacific Ocean, through a narrow waterway which we now call the Straits of Magellan. They had found a way through to the East!

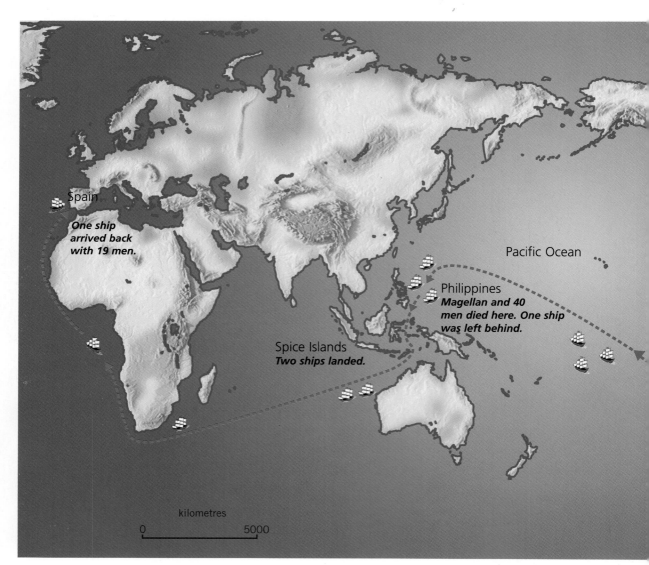

Spain

One ship arrived back with 19 men.

Pacific Ocean

Philippines
Magellan and 40 men died here. One ship was left behind.

Spice Islands
Two ships landed.

kilometres

0   5000

▼ One sailor, Antonio Pigafetta, kept a diary. Some years later he published it, which is how we know what happened on this voyage.

But then, one ship's crew deserted the rest and sailed off with most of the **fleet's** food. Magellan's men were so hungry they had to eat mouldy biscuits, and even rats and leather. Twenty men starved to death.

Disaster in the Philippines

They crossed the Pacific Ocean and landed in the Philippine Islands. There, Magellan got involved in a local quarrel, and was killed, along with 40 of his men. The crew who survived went on in two ships, leaving one behind. They finally arrived at the Spice Islands and loaded up with valuable spices.

Both ships set off for Spain, but one was captured by the Portuguese. The remaining ship arrived back in Spain in 1522. It had sailed right around the globe, but only 19 men had completed the journey. Magellan and his men had paid a high price for the new route they discovered.

Five ships set out.

Spain

Atlantic Ocean

One ship deserted with food supplies, 20 men died of hunger.

South America

One ship was wrecked here.

N

Straits of Magellan

◀ The route taken by Magellan's ships

Science and empire

Some sea voyages were made with scientific aims. The British **navigator** Captain James Cook was sent to the tropical island of Tahiti in 1769, to watch an event in space.

Tahiti was an ideal place to **observe** the planet Venus passing between the Earth and the Sun. **Astronomers** wanted to time how long it took Venus to pass across the Sun, as this measurement would help them to calculate the distance between the Earth and the Sun.

▲ Cook was involved in making maps on several of his voyages. Some of his maps were so accurate, they were still being used a hundred years later.

▼ The route taken by Captain Cook in the *Endeavour*. After visiting Tahiti, he explored much of the Pacific Ocean.

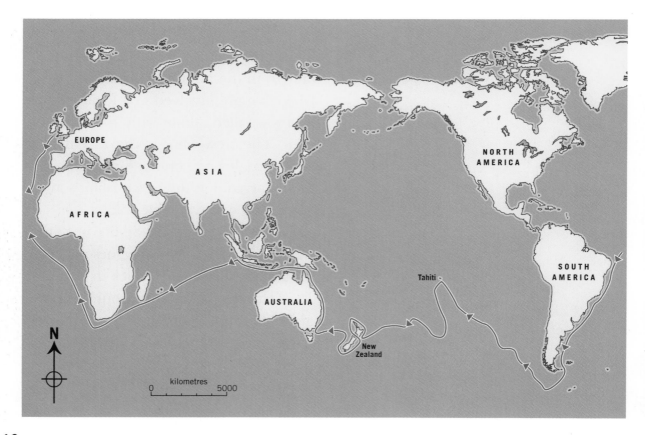

▼ Captain Cook's map of New Zealand. You can see how accurate it is by comparing it with a map of New Zealand in an atlas.

▲ These pictures of birds and a bat were drawn by one of Cook's nature experts on his voyage to Australia.

Secret orders

After the observation of Venus, Cook opened an envelope containing secret orders. He was told to sail on and explore the rest of the Pacific. He was asked to look for new lands, and to find out whether New Zealand was part of some massive **continent**.

The *Endeavour* sailed on to Australia, with the scientists aboard making maps and recording the wildlife. Botany Bay was given its name because the plant experts on board (botanists) found so many new kinds of plants there.

As a result of Cook's voyages, the government claimed some of the new lands as British **colonies**. British people started to move there, although the **native** people who were living there had no choice in the matter.

▲ A **replica** of the *Endeavour* has been built. It sails around the world, to different places connected with Cook.

Race into space

A lot of exploration has been done for political reasons. For example, Magellan's sponsors stood to gain over their enemies by having a new route to the Spice Islands. But perhaps the most famous example of two nations battling over possible discoveries is the story of the space race.

see *Magellan* p.8

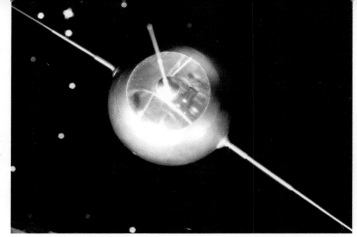

▲ In 1957, the USSR was the first into space with the unmanned craft *Sputnik 1*, showing that a spacecraft could be made to orbit the Earth.

In the 1950s, two great countries were **rivals**; each wanted to be the major power in the world. They were the United States of America (USA) and the Union of Soviet Socialist Republics (USSR), which was made up of Russia and countries around it. Each wanted to be the first to launch into space, in order to show the world that their technology was better.

Manned flights

In 1961, the USSR made the first manned flight: the **cosmonaut**, Yuri Gagarin, **orbited** the Earth in a spacecraft called *Vostok 1*.

In 1962, the US spacecraft *Friendship 7* orbited the Earth, piloted by the **astronaut** John Glenn. As he flew over Australia, all the houses in Perth switched their lights off, then on again, to say "hello" to him.

▼ The American astronauts returned to Earth by splashing down in the sea. The Soviet cosmonauts came down on the land.

5 The Command and Service Modules separated, the Command Module entered the Earth's atmosphere and used parachutes to slow its fall.

2 The Command and Service Modules, combined with the Lunar Module, orbited the Moon.

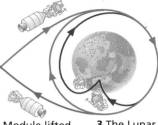

4 The Lunar Module lifted off the surface and rejoined the Command and Service Modules.

3 The Lunar Module separated and descended to the Moon's surface. The Command and Service Modules continued to orbit the Moon.

▲ The *Apollo* spacecraft took off and circled the Earth.

The Moon lander module separated from *Columbia*, the main craft, to land on the Moon.

Half of the Moon lander took the astronauts back to *Columbia*. The other half stayed on the Moon.

The part of *Columbia* containing the astronauts splashed down on Earth.

▲ To walk on the Moon, the astronauts Neil Armstrong and Buzz Aldrin wore special suits. These protected them from the cold and provided them with air to breathe, as the Moon has no atmosphere.

see Clothing p.27

To the Moon

Next, the two nations developed spacecraft that could take more than one person, and spacesuits to enable astronauts to go outside their craft in space. In 1966, both nations made unmanned landings on the Moon to check how suitable the surface was for landings.

Finally, Neil Armstrong and Buzz Aldrin, two astronauts from the US craft *Apollo 11*, landed on the Moon on 20 July 1969.

2 Exploring new ideas

Darwin

Physical exploration has sometimes triggered "**mental** exploration" in people's minds, and has changed their ideas about the world.

In 1831, a young clergyman called Charles Darwin was invited to join the ship Beagle, which was setting off on a five-year journey to map the coast of South America. The expedition needed a nature expert and Darwin agreed to go because he had always been a keen naturalist.

▲ In spite of his religious training, Darwin slowly gathered **evidence** for a theory which many people felt completely contradicted Christian teaching.

▼ The route taken by the *Beagle* round the coast of South America.

Galapagos Islands

COLOMBIA

EQUADOR

PERU

BRAZIL

SOUTH AMERICA

N

Pacific Ocean

South Atlantic Ocean

kilometres
0   2000

Darwin was astonished by the many different kinds of birds and plants they saw on the trip. He made a huge collection of plants and fossils.

In September 1835, the *Beagle* arrived at the Galapagos Islands, 1000 km off the coast of Ecuador. Here, Darwin recorded animals, birds and plants that could not be seen anywhere else. They seemed to have developed separately from the animals on the mainland, and this idea led Darwin towards his revolutionary new ideas about life on Earth.

The Origin of Species

Darwin started to realize that all the animals and plants in the world had developed, or evolved, over millions of years, to suit the places where they lived. This development would explain why creatures on an **isolated** island could be so different from the ones everywhere else.

In 1859, twenty years after he came home from the voyage, Darwin published a book called *The Origin of Species* setting out his theory of **evolution**. It caused a huge argument. People felt that Darwin's ideas went against the teaching of the Bible, which said that everything on the

▲ These iguanas only live on the Galapagos. They live partly on the land and partly in the sea.

Earth was created in six days and had never changed since. Today, many people accept Darwin's ideas, but in some places the argument continues.

▼ The Galapagos Islands are named after their most famous inhabitants, which are giant tortoises: "galapagos" means "tortoises" in Spanish.

Galileo and the Universe

Making a **mental** journey can sometimes be as dangerous as actually going on an **expedition**.

Galileo Galilei, a university teacher in Pisa in Italy, made a dangerous mental journey in the early 1600s. He was one of the "great thinkers" of his time, and he became convinced that the way people imagined the Universe to be was wrong. So he started to teach his students that, instead of being fixed in the middle of the Universe, the Earth moved around the Sun.

▼ Until Galileo's time, most Europeans believed that the Universe had the Earth fixed in the centre, and the Sun and all the planets moved around it.

▼ An **astronomer** called Copernicus thought that the Universe was actually like this. The Sun was at the centre and the Earth and all the other planets moved around the Sun.

Phases of Venus

Galileo watched the planet Venus and saw how it seemed to change shape – just as our Moon changes shape through the month. He was sure that this could only be explained by Venus moving around the Sun rather than around the Earth. And if Venus moved around the Sun, then so must everything else, including the Earth. So he started to teach this new theory to his students.

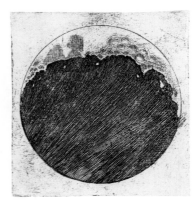

▲ Galileo used a telescope he had invented to explore the night sky, watching the stars and planets. What he saw convinced him that Copernicus was right.

This teaching got him into trouble with the Church, who did not agree with this view of the Universe. They ordered Galileo to stop teaching people that the Earth moves at all.

Galileo changed his teaching, but a few years later, in 1632, he published a book which discussed both versions of the Universe. The Church sentenced him to imprisonment for life, even after he agreed to say that he didn't believe the Earth moved.

The next year, he was released from prison, but was not allowed to leave his house. Galileo had lost his freedom just for trying to explain new ideas – ideas that are accepted everywhere today.

3 Preparing for an expedition

Funding

Unless they are very rich, all explorers have to find someone to **finance** their journeys: to pay for transport, food, equipment and all their other expenses.

see Columbus p.7

▲ Loading expedition supplies on a steamship at London docks in 1885.

▲ Columbus described his plans for his voyage to the rulers of Spain, Portugal, France and England, and asked for help, but he was refused by them all. Finally, he asked the King and Queen of Spain again, and eventually they agreed to **sponsor** his voyage.

Some explorers went in hope of prizes: in 1825, René Caillié won the prize for being the first Frenchman to travel across the Sahara desert to Timbuktu, and return.

Many explorers had to find private sponsorship, and so do many of today's adventurers. In 1909, Captain Scott approached the British Admiralty to fund his **expedition** to the South Pole. When they refused, he travelled around Britain, raising £40 000 in private sponsorship, which was a very large sum of money then.

see Scott p.19

Planning

Explorers have to plan carefully if their expeditions are to succeed. Planning and experience decided the fates of Robert Falcon Scott and Roald Amundsen in their race to the South Pole in 1911.

Amundsen was a Norwegian who had lived among the **Inuit** near the North Pole. He took husky dogs to drag the equipment. His team's clothes were made of warmth-trapping fur.

Scott and his team were not used to very low temperatures, and did not have enough warm clothing. Scott took horses, but these became exhausted and had to be shot. Then the men had to drag the sleds themselves.

Scott also changed the plans he had made for the final trek to the Pole. Instead of taking three men he took four, so their supplies ran out.

▲ Amundsen's dogs pulled the sleds and the men were towed along behind on skis.

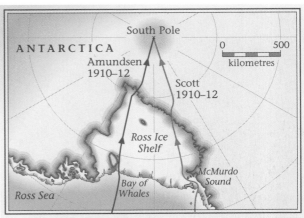

▲ The two routes to the Pole

▼ One of Scott's ill-fated ponies

Amundsen reached the South Pole on 14th December 1911, a month before Scott's team.

Scott and his men were bitterly disappointed to find Amundsen had reached the Pole first. Then blizzards overtook them. In March 1912, they died on the way back from the Pole, just 16 km from safety.

Quarrels and rivalry

A problem every team of explorers has to consider is the possibility of disagreements. Not every detail can be agreed in advance because exploration involves dealing with the "unknown". Sometimes partners end up as **rivals**. In 1857, Richard Burton and John Speke went to Africa to look for the **source** of the River Nile. Later, they had a huge argument.

▲ John Speke   ▲ Richard Burton

▼ The River Nile, and Speke and Burton's route

Burton fell ill on the journey, and Speke continued without him. Speke reached a huge lake, which he named Lake Victoria. He decided it was the source of the Nile, but he did not explore further and find definite proof.

When Speke announced his success, Burton accused him of not having any **evidence**. Speke said that Burton was jealous. They were probably both right!

The argument went on until 1864, when the two men were persuaded to **debate** the question in public. Speke died in a shooting accident the day before the debate, so their argument was never settled. Ten years later, an American, Henry Morton Stanley, found proof that Speke was right.

Crew members

An **expedition** has a better chance of succeeding if it has the right combination of people in the team. But choosing the people carefully is a relatively new idea.

At the time Columbus made his great voyage, a ship's crew was made up of anyone available in the port. There might be some experienced sailors, but it was a great opportunity for criminals on the run – who had no interest in the voyage except as a means of escape. This is one reason why explorers often had trouble with their crew, as Magellan did.

see Magellan p.9

▼ On long voyages, fights often broke out.

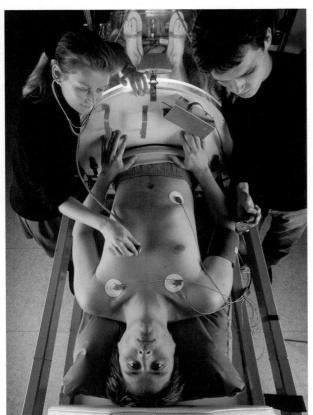

In contrast to this, the organizers of the space programme select the members of each mission with great care. The only people allowed to volunteer for the first US space missions were **test pilots** who also knew a lot about engineering. From the 500 who applied, only seven were selected for training.

◀ As part of their training, **astronauts** are put in machines like this to get used to the fast **acceleration** and weightlessness in rockets. Astronauts are also checked to make sure they are really fit and healthy.

see Race into space p.12

4 Equipment for explorers

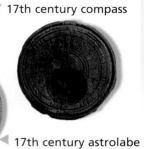

▼ 17th century compass

◀ 17th century astrolabe

▲ Early explorers relied on **astronomers** like this man to help them navigate.

Transport and navigation

Explorers have to use whatever transport is available for their journey.

Overland explorers have travelled on foot, by horse, by dog-sled in the polar regions, and by camel in the deserts. **Navigators** have explored lakes, rivers, and oceans by ship and have even taken submarines under the polar icecap! Pilots have reached remote places by aeroplane, helicopter, balloon and spacecraft.

Until the late 1600s, explorers had leaky, old ships. Someone who saw Magellan's fleet said it looked too rotten to put to sea. Captain Cook's ship, the *Endeavour*, was strong and seaworthy, but it was just a converted coal ship. A good ship was worth a lot of money, and no one was prepared to risk a valuable craft on a journey it might not return from.

Now, we put more effort into making sure the craft that set out not only return, but protect the people they carry. So most **vehicles** used by modern explorers are carefully designed to survive the journey.

Navigation

Navigators use a range of equipment to keep track of their position, course and speed.

For centuries, compasses have been used by travellers to check directions. With an accurate map and a compass it is not difficult to work out your route.

Navigators in Columbus's day used **astrolabes** like the one in the picture opposite. By measuring the position of a star or planet above the horizon, they could judge roughly how far from the poles they were, both on sea and land.

▲ Mini-submarines have increased the possibilities of exploring deep in the oceans. Two people can survive for up to five days in this **submersible**. It has been used for investigating ancient shipwrecks.

◀ The Space Shuttle has been designed to land like a plane, rather than splashing down in the sea when it returns from a flight in space.

Before speedometers, a log was used to check a ship's speed. A sailor would throw a **tethered** log overboard and count how many knots in the string went past in a minute. Ships' speedometers still measure speed in "knots" today, although they are electronic.

FACT

Many sailors and travellers now use electronic signals sent from artificial satellites. This Global Positioning System (GPS) tells them exactly where on the Earth they are.

Food and drink

The food available for explorers to take with them has changed dramatically over the years.

Until a hundred years ago, there were no fridges and only a few ways to preserve food. So the food that explorers could take on voyages then was quite limited. The meat was salted to stop it going bad, but vegetables could not be preserved.

→ see p.6

Water was also a problem. On a long voyage away from land, water became slimy and foul tasting. So sailors drank spirits instead, such as rum.

Because sailors did not have fresh fruit and vegetables to eat, many sailors died of scurvy, a disease that is caused by a shortage of vitamins.

▼ A dry biscuit, known as "hard tack", was standard sailors' food for many years.

FACT

Sailors experimented with different foods to try to prevent scurvy. These included pickled cabbage, fruit syrup, and marmalade made from carrots. But cooking destroys the vitamins in food. Captain Cook gave his men lime juice – and it worked! For years afterwards, British sailors ate limes on voyages, and were given the nickname "limeys".

→ see Science and empire p.10

Astronauts' food and drink needs to be eaten from sealed containers. This makes sure it does not fly around and stick to everything in weightless conditions.

▲ This is some of the food and cooking equipment taken to the South Pole by Scott in 1911.

Polar food

Pemmican is preserved meat made using a Cree Indian recipe. It is very concentrated, so a small amount provides a lot of energy. It was used by the Polar explorers in the early 1900s.

Space food

Astronauts now have a wide menu of food available to them, all specially prepared and packaged. Some of it is dried, but water can be added to make it almost like normal food. They have 75 different foods to choose from, plus 30 types of fruit and vegetables. There are also drinks, and even ketchup and mayonnaise.

Mountaineering food

On climbing **expeditions**, a lot of food and equipment has to be carried to the base camp by porters or pack animals. A variety of dried or concentrated food is now available for expeditions.

▲ The Himalayan Sherpa people, who live in Nepal, help travellers to transport heavy loads in the mountains.

Clothing

An explorer's clothing can make the difference between success and failure. Sometimes, this is important for protection from the weather, and sometimes for disguise.

Disguises

In 1853, Sir Richard Burton was one of the first westerners to visit the holy Muslim city of Mecca. He could speak the right languages, but he also had to disguise his appearance. If he had arrived in western clothes he would never have been allowed into the city.

▲ Alexandra David-Neel stained her face and hands with walnut juice to make them darker, and blackened her hair with ink.

▲ Richard Burton dressed himself in Arab clothes and took the name El Haj Abdullah, claiming to be a doctor from Afghanistan. Like this, he was able to visit the city without being caught. He claimed that it was not disrespectful, as at the time he was a practising Muslim.

In a similar way in 1923, Alexandra David-Neel disguised herself as a Tibetan peasant woman in order to visit the holy cities of Tibet. By pretending to be very ignorant, she made an excuse for not talking very much, which might have given her away.

Protective clothing

Wetsuits are designed to keep divers and sailors dry and warm. Warm fur clothing helped protect Amundsen and his men from the fierce cold of Antarctica. But the spacesuits worn by **astronauts** are the ultimate in protective clothing.

see Planning p.19

A spacesuit is very well padded for **insulation**: it is very cold in space. The backpack contains a life support system.

The visor on the helmet is plated with gold to protect the astronaut's eyes from the **radiation** from the Sun, which is much stronger in space than it is on Earth.

see Race into space p.13

Key
1. controls to keep the temperature in the suit steady
2. water
3. oxygen to breathe
4. electrical power and a radio to stay in touch with the ship or Earth

▲ Divers who explore wrecks wear wetsuits like these. An extra layer inside traps warmth.

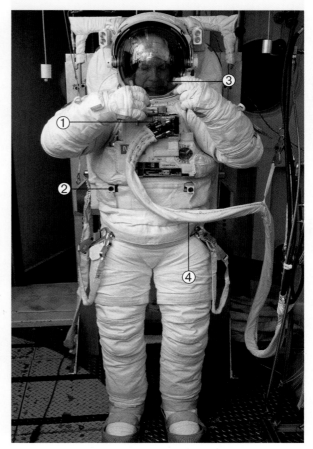

▲ Astronauts need to wear spacesuits with breathing apparatus whenever they go outside their craft.

5 Modern technology and new challenges

▲ Images of Jupiter (right) and Saturn (left) produced by *Voyager 2*

Controlling danger

In the modern world, people are very aware of the dangers of exploration, and leaders try to make sure that no lives are lost if possible. As most of the places that remain to be explored are dangerous for people to go into, new ways to explore them have been found, using instruments and cameras.

Exploring space

Other planets are too far away to send people to them. The journeys can take many years and would be very dangerous. So exploration in space is now mostly done by **unmanned** probes, controlled by computers.

In 1977, the two *Voyager* craft went to take pictures of the outer planets. They went to Jupiter in 1979, and on to Saturn. *Voyager 2* arrived at Uranus in 1986 and Neptune in 1989.

Both *Voyager* craft finally went off into space, never to return to Earth. An advantage of unmanned craft is that they don't have to come back.

Exploring under the sea

Unmanned craft called Remotely Operated Vehicles (ROVs), and Autonomous Underwater Vehicles (AUVs), are used in underwater exploration. These craft can go into places where even people in submarines and special diving suits cannot safely go.

Pollution

One of the effects of exploration is that newcomers have introduced new diseases into areas they have visited, causing the deaths of many of the **native** people. Pollution is another problem, even in space. It is already littered with abandoned satellites and parts of rockets.

▲ The AUV *Odyssey 2* was sent under the Arctic in 1996 to study how ice and sea water react together. This information is useful for predicting global warming. In Antarctica, scientists are preparing to explore a huge freshwater lake under the ice, using specially designed instruments. It is vital that they do not introduce any pollution into this untouched zone.

▼ A test model of an unmanned Mars rover

Testing ourselves

Exploration has always involved finding out about new things and places. But now explorers have been to most of the places where people can go, they are undertaking new sorts of challenges: to test what people are really able to do.

Back-up teams, radio and video links, and people monitoring the explorers' progress help to reduce the risks involved in modern exploration. But the spirit of adventure is still there, as it was for Columbus and Magellan who wondered, "Is it possible to do this?" Explorers want to try.

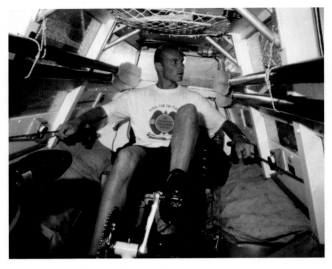

▲ The *Moksha* pedal boat is part of an ongoing attempt to travel right round the World using only human power.

▼ In 1999, the two pilots of the *Breitling Orbiter 3* made the first non-stop balloon flight around the world.

Glossary

acceleration Speeding up.

astrolabe An instrument to help sailors steer by the stars.

astronaut A space traveller.

astronomer Someone who watches stars and planets and tries to understand the universe.

colony Land that people from another country settle in and control.

continent A large land mass, like America, Australia or Antarctica.

cosmonaut A space traveller from Russia or the USSR.

debate A discussion.

evidence Proof, things that show an idea is true.

evolution Gradual change into something different.

expedition A journey of exploration or discovery.

finance To pay for something.

fleet A group of ships.

insulation Keeping heat in and cold out.

Inuit Inuit people live in the far north, near the North Pole.

isolated Far from anywhere else.

mental In the mind.

native Belonging in a country or place.

navigation Instruments and skills for knowing where you are and finding a route.

navigator A sea explorer, the person who finds the route.

observe To watch carefully and make notes.

orbit To go right round the world in space.

radiation Light, heat and other energy put out by the Sun.

replica An exact copy.

rival A person who competes against someone else.

source The place where a river starts from.

sponsor To pay for.

submersible A craft that can travel underwater.

test pilots People who fly new kinds of planes to check if they work properly in the air.

tethered With string or rope tied to it.

trade route A way to get to and from places where you can find things to buy and sell.

unmanned With no people on board.

vehicle A craft.

Books for further reading

Beyond the horizons: Magellan and Da Gama by Clint Twist (Evans Brothers 1993)

Exploration through the ages: the voyages of Captain Cook by Richard Humble (Franklin Watts 1990)

Explorers and discoverers by Neil Grant (BBC Factfinders 1992)

Famous explorers by Daniel Rogers (Wayland 1993)

I was there: Christopher Columbus by J.D. Clare (Bodley Head 1992)

The Usborne book of explorers: from Columbus to Armstrong by Felicity Everett and Struan Reid (Usborne 1991)

Women and travel by Dea Birkett (Wayland 1993)

Index